SLEEPLESS FOR SOCIETY

Abhijit Naskar is the twenty-first century Neuroscientist whose contributions in Cognitive and Behavioral Neuroscience have helped the world tackle the issues of mental illness, prejudice, hate, extremism, discrimination and segregation more effectively. As an untiring advocate of mental health and universal acceptance, he became a beloved best-selling author all over the world with his very first book "The Art of Neuroscience in Everything". With his pioneering ventures into the Neuropsychology of beliefs and biases, he has hugely contributed in the eradication of religious and cultural differences in our world, for which he is popularly hailed as the humanitarian scientist, who takes the human civilization in the path of sweet general harmony.

SLEEPLESS
FOR SOCIETY

ABHIJIT NASKAR

Also by Abhijit Naskar

The Art of Neuroscience in Everything
Your Own Neuron: A Tour of Your Psychic Brain
The God Parasite: Revelation of Neuroscience
The Spirituality Engine
Love Sutra: The Neuroscientific Manual of Love
Homo: A Brief History of Consciousness
Neurosutra: The Abhijit Naskar Collection
Autobiography of God: Biopsy of A Cognitive Reality
Biopsy of Religions: Neuroanalysis towards Universal
Tolerance
Prescription: Treating India's Soul
What is Mind?
In Search of Divinity: Journey to The Kingdom of Conscience
Love, God & Neurons: Memoir of a scientist who found
himself by getting lost
The Islamophobic Civilization: Voyage of Acceptance
Neurons of Jesus: Mind of A Teacher, Spouse & Thinker
Neurons, Oxygen & Nanak
The Education Decree
Principia Humanitas
The Krishna Cancer
Rowdy Buddha: The First Sapiens
We Are All Black: A Treatise on Racism
The Bengal Tigress: A Treatise on Gender Equality
Either Civilized or Phobic: A Treatise on Homosexuality
Wise Mating: A Treatise on Monogamy
Illusion of Religion: A Treatise on Religious
Fundamentalism
The Film Testament
Human Making is Our Mission: A Treatise on Parenting
I Am The Thread: My Mission
7 Billion Gods: Humans Above All
Lord is My Sheep: Gospel of Human
Morality Absolute
A Push in Perception
Let The Poor Be Your God
Conscience over Nonsense
Saint of The Sapiens
Time to Save Medicine
Fabric of Humanity

Build Bridges not Walls: In the name of Americana
The Constitution of The United Peoples of Earth
Lives to Serve Before I Sleep
When Humans Unite: Making A World Without Borders
All For Acceptance
Monk Meets World
Mission Reality
Citizens of Peace: Beyond The Savagery of Sovereignty
Operation Justice: To Make A Society That Needs No Law
See No Gender
The Gospel of Technology
Every Generation Needs Caretakers: The Gospel of
Patriotism
Aşkanjali: The Sufi Sermon
Mad About Humans: World Maker's Almanac
Revolution Indomable
When Call The People: My World My Responsibility
No Foreigner Only Family
Hurricane Humans: Give me accountability, I'll give you
peace
Ain't Enough to Look Human
Servitude is Sanctitude
Time To End Democracy: The Meritocratic Manifesto
I Vicdansaadet Speaking: No Rest Till The World is Lifted
Boldly Comes Justice: Sentient not Silent
Good Scientist: When Science and Service Combine

DEDICATION

*This book is dedicated to those who are mad
enough to die for justice and inclusion.*

CONTENTS

1.   The Very First Step

Inability to recognize reality is not insight, it's blindness - this is what I stated in "Good Scientist". And this is the very foundation on which our current discourse is going to take place. You know me most probably as an activist for international harmony and inclusion, even though I do not define myself as an activist, for what I do is not activism, it's plain, ordinary humanity - and this plain, ordinary humanity does not require extraordinary titles. However, I accept the pedestal on which you have placed me, even though I prefer the ground over the pedestal.

My role as a scientist in the society has been to point out the subtleties of human nature while directing it in a civilized course. And to direct the human society in a civilized course, it is imperative that you do not lose touch with the reality of the present in the illusive pursuit of an insane, futuristic dream. A dream can be as insane as you want it to be, but if you turn blind to the present altogether and go into denial of the current reality, then nothing can make that dream come true, whether it is insane or not.

I have a dream as well - my dream is that all humans will one day stand as one, crossing the bounds of race, religion, nationality, gender and sexuality. But mere dreaming doesn't make a dream come true, for the lifeforce of a dream is action - and that action must be based upon the present. You must have your feet firmly placed on the grounds of the present with your eyes gazing at a distant and almost invisible future. Thus we ought to act if we are to make that invisible future visible.

I dream of a future without conflicts - without war - without the loss of lives due to petty old tribalism. In short I dream of a future without armed intervention. Here some may ask the question - is it a rational dream - and my reply is, a rational dream is never a dream. So the question is not can we build a world without conflicts - the real question is, should be build a world without conflicts! Now the answer appears in our mind much easier - doesn't it! Once we have a clear perception of whether we should build a world without conflicts, then we can proceed with the investigation on what we can do to make it happen.

2. **Plight of A Humanitarian**
   (The Sonnet)

6

Plight of A Humanitarian
(The Sonnet)

My dear people of earth,
I die everyday so that your children can live.
My dear people of earth,
You've been selfish for long now it's time to give.
My dear people of earth,
I struggle everyday with your interest on top.
My dear people of earth,
Enough of this tribalism now it's time to grow up.
My dear people of earth,
I'm really tired and weary righting all wrong.
My dear people of earth,
Join me in making a world where we all belong.
I promise I don't want much from you.
All I ask is that you bid your sectarianism adieu.

3. Treatment of Terror and Conflicts

I do not like guns - but how can this dislike - a simple, ordinary, everyday dislike build a world without guns? The straightforward answer is - it cannot. Guns are inhuman, but even more inhuman is the unwillingness to take up guns and facilitate the murder of innocent lives in the hands of angry, unstable, misguided terrorists. That's where the armed forces come in.

Some couch philosophers and shallow peace advocates often argue that it is never okay to kill people - they are angry, they are misguided, they need help - and this argument would indeed be accurate if we lived in an ideal world - but the harsh reality of the matter is that we do not. Our world is not ideal - it is infested with issues that sometimes compel us to choose between two options, both of which are inhuman - but one of them is far more inhuman that the other.

However, in these circumstances though we may choose the less inhuman path, at the same time we must work towards alleviating the societal issues that breed the inhumanity we are trying to prevent. There will always be some people who will be angry and unstable, but we can reduce their number exponentially if we just actually, genuinely start working on eliminating the breeding ground of terror - and the breeding ground of terror is inequality – it is disparity.

Killing terrorists doesn't end terrorism, it only postpones it. To end terrorism we have to end inequality. And to end inequality the civilized humans from all corners of the society must stand up and act with accountability. And do not bother with whether it is possible to end inequality or not - an illogical yet humane step towards an impossible future is a thousand times better than a logical yet inhuman step towards a possible future.

Remember, it is through many such impossible struggles that we have become the masters of an entire planet - logically speaking, there's no reason why the humans should have achieved that position, yet we have - so our very existence is evidence of an impossible future. Let me make it even simpler for you. Forget the humankind - take me in its place. I don't have a college degree, I don't come from money or from an academic family, I didn't have any resourceful acquaintance to speak of, yet today I am at the forefront of humankind's struggle for inclusion, justice and equality.

All I had was a vision and an unending persistence. Each failure made me even more stubborn towards my vision - each failure gave me an inexplicable bliss that carried me further. And eventually they led me where I am today. So the point is, forget the argumentation of logic over what is possible and what is not - action in the course of humaneness should be our prime directive, not argumentation.

Killing people is wrong, but more wrong is to stand by while those people continue to take the lives of others. And those who do not appreciate the soldiers, that is, the armed forces, and instead pompously talk about peace, should try to live a single day without the soldiers. Erase the soldiers and you'll give power to terror - erase the teachers and you'll give power to ignorance - erase the doctors and you'll give power to sickness - erase the scientists and you'll give power to regress.

The point is, terror has no nationality, it has no religion, it has no gender - its nationality is ignorance, its religion is bigotry, its gender is intolerance. And if you are able to read my words right now, it is made possible by those soldiers who have given up their everyday pleasures in their fight against terror so that you can live your life with all its sweetness and colors.

Armed forces may not be a moral solution to conflicts, it is nevertheless a necessary one - and it pains me to admit this, that even with all the humanitarian endeavors from individuals as well as governments across the world in the course of world peace, we will still need some sort of armed forces to defend humanity against the atrocities of bigotry-induced terror, because no matter how internationally inclusive and humane we turn our society there will always be some unstable yobos who won't be happy with inclusion, secularism and unification. These unstable creatures have nothing to do with any particular religion, they can come from all religions and backgrounds, even the textually most noble ones.

This is the price we pay for democracy, where we leave human behavior to human will - law applies to the humans only when their behavior endangers others in some way, but till then, your behavior is your business. This is at the same time a boon and a curse of democracy. It's a boon because you are free to do whatever you like with your life, and it's also a curse because a great deal of society's wellbeing depends on individual accountability. If one person goes off the rockers and commits something horrible, no law can undo that horror - law can punish it surely, but it can't bring back the lives lost or undo the harm done because of the acts of one reckless individual.

The purpose of law is to punish inhumanity, whereas the purpose of armed forces is to prevent inhumanity. And to punish inhumanity is quite easy, but to prevent inhumanity takes far greater resolve. It's not something that anybody can achieve. Anybody can achieve the things that are easy. Good people are here to solve the tough problems of society.

And the tough problems of society are not merely the responsibility of the government and the armed forces, they are the responsibility of each and every human being on earth. In fact, only when all humans regardless of their personal problems of life give their best to solve the issues of society can those issues be solved at all. Let's take border patrol for example.

Border patrol is relevant so long as there is the issue of illegal immigration, and illegal immigration persists so long as there are oppression, persecution and scarcities in society. Nobody wants to leave their homeland illegally out of their heart's desire, they are compelled to do so as the last resort due to utter degradation of life there.

So to reduce border patrol we have to put an end to illegal immigration - and though we may not be able to put an absolute end to illegal immigration, we can reduce it exponentially - and to reduce illegal immigration each nation has to work on its problems and all other privileged nations must help them do so. This means that not just the government but you the individual must work to solve those problems of your nation and the governments and citizens of other nations must help in that endeavor. This is not an obligation, this is plain, ordinary humanity.

4.   Future without Armed Conflicts

Armed forces exist due to the indifference of the people towards the troubles of society - once the people wake up and act, with or without governmental intervention, all armed forces will soon turn (almost) obsolete, because other than taking care of rare few acts of terror they would have nothing else to do. But this won't happen merely with talk, for it would require an absolute over-hall of the very paradigm that facilitates the birth of terror.

Quite like education, with armed forces as well we are stuck with an ancient paradigm - a paradigm that is not compatible with the needs of an exponentially globalizing human society. We are stuck with a rugged model that sustains nationalist animosity instead of working in the course of international unity.

The concept of international relations is actually code for international separatism. Its purpose is not to facilitate discussion but to sustain debates. No party in these debates cares about truth or peace or unification, all they care about is their exclusive personal security. And so long as states care about national security, international security will always remain a myth.

I am not saying that matters of national security should be abandoned altogether, instead what I am suggesting is that each nation has to get its priorities straight first - and the highest priority of each nation should be international unity, not national security. Once the nations can genuinely engage in interventions of international unity, national security will prevail on its own.

To achieve this, we must reform our very notion of nationalism - the purpose of nationalism in a civilized, global society must be to pave the course of internationalism, or else, no amount of peace talks can ensure world peace. Soldiers will continue to die due to our savagery - mothers and fathers will continue to lose their kids because of our stupidity - husbands and wives will continue to lose their spouses because of our foolishness - children will continue to lose their parents because of our appalling indifference. This cannot go on - this must not go on.

And remember, governments won't care to put an end to this insanity, for they only have a few years of power - so they don't have much time for actually serving the interest of the people.

The people must take it upon themselves to do what's best for their society, for their nation, for their world - for our world. What can you do you ask - simple - do your part to lift your society. It won't happen overnight, but the work must begin now in the hands of everyday responsible humans, or else nothing will change.

Remembering the martyrs and honoring the armed forces on veterans day may make you feel proud, but sustaining a tradition that conditions you to celebrate the loss of life in the name of patriotism is not something to take pride in - if anything this celebration is a brutal reminder of tribalism - of our shortfalls - of our inability to assimilate - of our failure in becoming truly civilized. Therefore, the need of the hour is, we work so that we no longer need a veterans day.

Whenever there is armed conflict somewhere in the world you stick to the TV channels as if you are watching a baseball game, then after a while you get bored and switch over to something more interesting. That's what the sacrifice of the soldiers mean to you - they are just content - that's what the sacrifice of the scientists, doctors and nurses mean to you - they are just content -

that's what the sacrifice of the activists mean to you - they are just content - and with such attitude flowing through the very veins of society no United Nations can bring peace into this world - to do that, you must change - every single being of character must change - every single being with compassion must change - every single one of us - with no exception - only then, perhaps - just perhaps, we will successfully put an end to the age-old tribalistic conflicts that have been choking our society to death all this time.

Throw away such nationalism that makes you a bigot - throw away such fundamentalism that makes you intolerant - throw away such intellectualism that makes you cold - throw away every single trace of separation from the fabric of your being and stand up fortified with the resuscitating flame of humility and oneness - stand up for your family and for the countless other families of our world - destroy your arrogance - demolish your prejudice - abolish all that is cruel and primitive in you - trample them all with your brave footsteps of conscience - and rise above - rise above them, to be the maker of a humane society for your children - to be the builder of an inclusive world for your children - to be the cornerstone of a civilized planet for all of future humanity - only and only if you can do that, then my friend - you can raise your head high and shout out loud to the world with your last breath - I am a human and I have lived as a human.

5.   When Calls Democracy

Just because there are soldiers dying so that you could live, it doesn't relieve you of your duty as a living human, just like handing over the responsibility of your country to a good leader doesn't make you free from your responsibilities as a living citizen. Let's take leadership in our United States for example.

The first step of good democracy is to choose a good leader, or more importantly, to not choose an animal as a leader - yet we made that ghastly mistake in 2016 by electing the most non-presidential creature on earth as the leader of our United States of America. There are good presidents, there are not so good presidents, but the unique problem with the president that we chose in the previous election was that it was not even a civilized human to begin with - it was an "it" not a he or she or they, and even after being handed over the very lives of the people that savage beast showed no sign of accountability whatsoever.

Thus, we broke our democracy in 2016, but with sheer determination and conscientious persistence we have succeeded in fixing that mistake. Yes, I am filled with joy unspeakable to say out loud, that we have corrected our mistake and fixed the democracy into its usual imperfect but functional state. I say imperfect because democracy by nature is not perfect, but the problem we created last time was that we took things too far, and in the process turned a somewhat functional democracy into an absolutely dysfunctional one - in short, we broke it. And had the leader we chose been a smart one, that is, if that idiot had been not an idiot, but an actual cunning dictator, we wouldn't be celebrating our victory as a civilized people today, instead we would be mourning the burial of democracy.

Fortunately, the insane ravings of a brainless, spineless and heartless maniac will no longer have to be considered as the statements originating from the sacred office of the President of the United States of America. We have fixed the broken democracy - yes - but the problems that existed before the maniac came to power still exist today. Therefore, we may cherish the restoration of our democracy as much as we want, the real work begins now. Choosing a proper human as a President doesn't magically make the problems of our nation disappear - those problems still exist - and they'll continue to give us chills time and again, unless we as a people stand accountable, both the government and the citizenry alike, and start working on those problems. Remember, the United States of America is not the responsibility of merely the President, the Vice President and their administration, it is the responsibility of each and every one of us whose veins carry the spirit of liberty and whose nerves carry the torrents of bravery.

We have won the battle of making the White House human again, but the war has just begun - the war against systemic racism, against misogyny, against homophobia, against islamophobia, against gun violence, and against post-pandemic health and economic crisis. So, though we may celebrate the victory for a short while, we mustn't lose sight of the issues - we must now actually start working as one people - as the American people to heal the wounds on the soul of our land of liberty. It's time to once again start dreaming and working towards the impossible dream - the dream of freedom not oppression, the dream of assimilation not discrimination, and above all, the dream of ascension not descension. Never forget my friend, AMERICA means Affectionate, Merciful, Egalitarian, Responsible, Inclusive, Conscientious and Accepting.

6. **Sonnet of Social Justice**

Sonnet of Social Justice

Get ready to fight,
Not with hate but accountability.
Get ready to fight,
Not with vengeance but humanity.
Get ready to speak,
Not as a cynic but as a sapiens.
Get ready to speak,
Crossing all egotistical grievance.
Get ready to stand,
Trampling all petty separation.
Get ready to stand,
Not in rebellion but in inclusion.
When it is too dark around,
Look inside for you're the light all round.

7.   Exploits of An Organic Species

36

Our world is not perfect- no organic world ever is - but taking pride in its shortcomings is not a sign of progress and civilization, it's a sign of hypocrisy and savagery. We must not reject those shortcomings either, nor should we ignore them, but we must recognize them for what they are, that is, shortcomings and then we can work towards correcting them. The first step of social development is the recognition of the prevailing issues of society.

Then comes the madness for development and justice. I am mad - I am loco - I am loco for society - I am loco for humanity - I am loco for universal unity - and till the last breath in my body I'll work to make that universal unity a reality, regardless of whether I fail or not - where I leave off, someone else as loco as me will pick up and where they leave off, others will pick. This is the way of change - this is the way of progress - and above all, this is the way of upliftment.

Society doesn't become better with mockery and ridicule - society becomes better when you take it upon yourself to make it better no matter the consequences. Do you remember the first time you fell in love - do you remember the sleeplessness it caused you - do you remember the restlessness it caused you - now think about this - do you feel the same kind of sleeplessness, the same kind of restlessness for the sufferings of society! If not, why not! You are a human, aren't you - you have blood in your veins, don't you - you have electricity in your nerves, don't you - but what's the point of having all this power, this magnificent, life-giving power, if it doesn't make you feel one with the society - what's the point of all this my friend - don't answer me - don't criticize yourself - don't judge yourself, just think - just ask yourself, what keeps you from feeling the sufferings of your society as your own!

If something happens to your partner, or your spouse, or your child, you go mad, then why do you not go mad when your society is in agony! Why not my friend! What the world needs is the fire of responsibility to stir up vigor and valor in the veins of the everyday, ordinary individuals of society. Not politician - not soldier - not scientist - not philosopher - not a professional of any kind - but a human being - a human being with the fire of accountability - that's what the world is desperately craving for. And that human - that majestic, life-giving, torch-bearing, vigorous human - is not going to fall from the sky - for it is nobody else but you. Remember, it's better to be loco for something, than to be sane for nothing - so become mad - become insane - go absolutely bonkers - for the society - for the community - for the world - because madness for humanity is true sanity, and sanity through indifference is utter insanity.

I do not care whether you are at peace or not, all I know is that there are countless innocent lives who are suffering due to the lack of the very essentials of life, the essentials that you take for granted - for them peace of mind is no more relevant than the affairs on an alien planet - do something to alleviate their suffering and you'll attain all the peace in the world. Seek peace, peace will disappear, seek purpose, peace will appear.

8.   Either Nationalist or Human

42

In the course of finding peace for the self as well as the society, the first step is to step outside the savage cage of tribalism, which is popularly known as nationalism. It is this simple. You can either be a nationalist or you can be a human, not both, because though in the old days nationalism aided the movement of national integrity and self-determination across the world, today it has become a filthy weapon in the exploits of bigotry, ignorance, narcissism and separatism.

Now, on paper you may find a rather ideal, pompous and naïve definition of nationalism, but we humans do not live on paper - we live in a real life - a life infested with real organic troubles that have no ideal solution - we must look at those troubles and try to solve them as we go along, by the use of our own mental faculties.

I am not advocating for globalism - I am not protesting against nationalism - all I am saying - we are humans above everything else and it's time we start living as such. You can call this simple act globalism, you can call it humanism, you can call it socialism, you can call it secularism, you can call it universalism - you can label it however you like - plenty are the tastes and plenty are the labels - the labels are irrelevant - the act is all-important.

I am truth and though different people name me differently across the world based on their taste and understanding, the sentiments and the intentions behind those names remain the same - they remain universal. The sun gives the same warmth across the world, though people call the sun differently (not to be taken literally, for different parts of the world have different level of exposure to the sun).

The individual's peace lies in the peace of the collective, and the peace of the collective lies in the actions of the individual. Peace of the collective cannot be produced by organizations, it can only be produced by the actions of the individuals - not tribal individuals mark you, but human individuals.

I am not asking you to get rid of your entire cultural identity, for no matter how much we try none of us can do that - but we must find a way to sustain our cultural identity without jeopardizing our humanity. Culture should be a path, not a prison. Every culture of this planet is teeming with magnificence, with sweetness, with majesty, and so long as you remain caged in the illusive supremacy and gravitas of your own culture you can never taste that great, grand universal existence.

The seed of cultural harmony lies not in the culture you are born in but in the recognition of the sweetness of other cultures. When other cultures become as sweet as that of the one that is imposed on you by society, that's when a true human is born. Then all cultures become your own culture - all countries become your own country - all religions become your own religion. And that my friend is the definition of humanity. Humanity is not a tribe - humanity is not a sect - humanity is not a theoretical ideal - humanity is the very force of liberty - humanity is the very fervor of piety - humanity is the very lifeforce of unity.

9. The Seed of Unity

What is unity - how is it born? Unity is not born of intellect - unity is not born of cynicism – and more importantly, unity is not born of logic. We are manifestations of the same force of nature. But the question is, can you feel this fact in your bones, like you feel the warmth of the sun on your skin!

A thousand facts are useless if the individual cannot realize them in real life. Do you feel that you belong to the world as much as you belong to your country - do you feel that you belong to the society as much as you belong to your family - do you feel that you belong to humanity as much as you belong to your community! It is this simple - until the world becomes one community, global harmony will remain a myth.

Globalism is a concept, a harsh, cold, tasteless concept - and we can never unite an organic species with such cold, mechanical, inorganic concepts - a species can be united only with sentiments - sentiments guided by humane conscience in the course of humanhood. True practical globalism is acceptance in action - it is inclusion in action - it is love in action. That's why I say, I haven't come for science, I have come for love. In love lies oneness - in love lies harmony - in love lies proper warm progress.

Remember this my friend - the breath of one is the breath of all - the life of one is the life of all. Don't theorize it - don't philosophize it - just feel it - feel it in your heart, in your veins, in your bones and in your nerves - feel it and once you truly do, action will rise from you on its own. Till the feeling of unity engulfs your being, no one and nothing can force action out of you - you will remain asleep in indifference till kingdom come.

Where there is love, there is action. And lack of action is actually lack of love. What this means is that indifference is a sign of lovelessness. When you love someone, you don't need to study philosophy or theology to rush in action whenever the person you love is in distress. Action comes naturally to you when you love.

But when it comes to the affairs of society all you do is argue over philosophies and theories without a single action to accompany them with – why - because you do not feel the love for the society, that you feel for your loved ones. And why not I ask you? Ask yourself - why not? And keep asking till the very question disappears from your mind and a sense of all-pervading love engulfs your soul.

10. The True Face of Luxury

Everything that's worth anything in the world has been achieved by the inquiring mind full of questions, not by those full of rituals and prejudice. Once you learn to question, you will start to learn. Nothing great is ever achieved through obedience and complacency. The more complacent you are, the more luxuries you desire, and the more luxuries you have, the more complacent you become. And all these comfort and luxuries aid in the manufacture of a comatose population.

I wish I could tell you that all the comfort and luxuries in the world are a sign of progress, but they are not - they are a sign of disparities - and these disparities can only go away with our sacrifice - with the sacrifice of the humanitarians - some must give all, all must give some, only then will there be actual civilized, sane, healthy and whole progress - progress that includes all of humanity, not just the privileged few.

Let me make this point clear further. Elon Musk's attempt to colonize Mars means absolutely nothing for those who can't even afford two wholesome meals a day, who are constantly living in fear of being bombed upon, who have no secure roof over their head. Space exploration is necessary, but I am not concerned with that, for my work is with the helpless and destitute, and I call upon the human in you to rise and do whatever is in your power to alleviate their real-life suffering. Netflix can wait, not the suffering of the helpless.

I hold all of you a traitor till you start doing your part for those in misery. What gives you the right to call yourself a human, till you feel for the humans - what gives you the right to call yourself a human, till you think for the humans - what gives you the right to call yourself a human, till you act for the humans!

We don't become human by wearing suits, we become human by handing over the clothes from our back to someone shivering in cold. We don't become human by eating at fancy restaurants, we become human by sharing the food on our plate with the homeless person across the street. We don't become human by flying first class in airplanes, we become human by lending our old jalopy to our neighbor so that they can take their ailing loved one to the hospital.

Human is a short word that goes a long way. And more importantly it is an ever-evolving word. Yesterday's humans were less human and more animal, today's humans are a bit more human than them but no less animal, and tomorrow's humans will be a bit more human and hopefully less animal than us. But this fact is nothing to be taken for granted, because in this very evolution - in this very ceaseless reformation lies the seed of a growing civilization. The moment this evolution stops, we as a species will start going downhill towards imminent catastrophe.

We are all a fusion of good and bad, and the only way forward is to empower the good and moderate the bad. Let me elaborate. I cannot do calculus, I do not understand quantum mechanics, my work is with human nature, and as such I can tell you precisely how good or bad humans are capable of being - despite that, I choose to believe and empower the good in a human while being mindful of the bad - even if there is one percent of goodness left in a person, then empowering that one percent is more civilized than criticizing the rest ninety-nine percent - the same holds true for a society - even if there is one percent of a population who are trying to do good, then empowering those one percent would achieve a thousand times more than criticizing the rest of the population.

Criticizing the weak doesn't erase their weakness, it only worsens it - and moreover, criticizing is the very sign of a weak character - the strong empowers the weak by walking alongside them till they foster strength and start walking on their own. Strength is a fascinating character, we don't become strong by discouraging others or by mocking others - we become strong ourselves by empowering others, by encouraging others - and by belittling others we only belittle ourselves.

11. Raising A Sentient World

The strength of the individual lies in the strength of the collective and the strength of the collective lies in strength of the individual - so prejudice of one individual becomes the prejudice of the collective and the prejudice of the collective breeds more prejudice in the individuals, unless the chain of prejudicial contagion is severed by the individual.

The same is with bigotry, the same is with racism, the same is with discrimination. Then there is one more such phenomenon which we call pride, the role of which in society is not as straightforward as we make it, quite like racism. In fact, pride can fuel racism if we are unaware of our biases.

There are two prides in the world, one that blinds you and the other that strengthens inter-human bond. There is no distinctive line between the two, in fact, in most cases they overlap each other, and that's precisely where the trouble begins. That's why it is imperative that you do not let pride drive you without the intervention of conscience.

Don't be a slave to pride, use pride as a tool to strengthen the bond with others, not to create more separations. Let me make it simpler still. Take pride in individuals, not in labels - not in labels of religion, not in labels of nationality, not in labels of party, not even in labels of intellect, philosophy and schools of thought.

I can take pride in an individual with potential from a remote corner of Africa - I can take pride in an individual with potential from a remote village in the balkans - I can take pride in an individual with potential from an underdeveloped south american neighborhood - but never in nationality, religion, ideology or philosophy.

I am a human and I love humans - I am a human and I take pride in humans. It's the people that add colors to the world, it's the people that add melodies to the world, it's the people that add sweetness to the world. In short, it's the people that add life to the world. Sentience of the world comes from the sentience of the individual - if the individual is prejudiced, if the individual is bigoted, if the individual is savage, then the world is bound to be prejudiced - it's bound to be bigoted - it's bound to be savage. So it all starts with the individual, it all starts with you.

Acknowledge your mistakes, acknowledge your errors and move past them.

Wise individuals have recorded their past so that fools can meet their tomorrow. Fools justify their mistakes, the wise recognize and correct their mistakes - that makes all the difference between human behavior and animal behavior. And more importantly that makes all the difference between the rise and fall of civilization.

The integrity of a civilization is predicated on our willingness to acknowledge our mistakes and work past them, instead of justifying them with all sorts of poppycock logic. Mistakes are healthy, for we learn a great deal of our capacities from our mistakes, but denial of mistakes is not just unhealthy, but downright lethal for the self as well as society. Making mistakes is neither human nor animal, it's just nature, but a human recognizes those mistakes and works to correct them while an animal on the other hand boasts those mistakes. And this holds true for not just mistakes but all shortcomings of human character.

For example, we humans occasionally have various impulses and often we act on those impulses without thinking. And a world where the humans act on impulses is only a kingdom of good-looking wild animals, not a civilized society of thinking humans. There are times when I feel like shouting certain things aloud out of sheer impulse, but reason and conscience keep me from doing so.

Not all thoughts and assumptions that appear in our mind are rational or humane. I am mentioning this particularly to point out that no one is infallible to prejudice, even if one happens to be a smarty-pants. So, the only way forward - the only humane way forward - the only civilized way forward is to be aware of one's impulses and keep them in check.

12. The Hard Problem of Inhumanity

You can have either a beautiful world with flaws or you can have a flawless world but cold. I choose the former, what would you choose? These flaws include those that are acceptable part of the human character and those that are downright inhuman - those that are downright animal behavior. And our struggle as a species is against this inhumanity.

That's why, the only hard problem I'm concerned with is the problem of inhumanity (for the hard problem of consciousness no longer exists) and the only way to solve it is to work with an uncorrupted concern for society in the course of inclusion and assimilation, no matter our field of work.

Whatever community we belong to, our highest priority must be to work towards an inclusive humanity. And those who have doubt whether we can achieve it at all, to them I say, we are new humans, there is nothing we cannot do. We are the generation assimilation - each footstep of ours will cause a tsunami of inclusion and acceptance all around us - a tsunami that is indomitable, a tsunami that is unstoppable.

There is a path from one heart to another that you cannot see with eyes. All know of this path, they have heard stories about it, but very few walk it. And they don't walk it because it's not luxurious, it's not sophisticated, and more importantly it's not visible to the eyes. To envision the path between hearts you must close your eyes and awaken your soul, and once you do you'll see you are the path yourself as well the pedestrian.

Close your eyes and you'll witness the world beyond worlds - close your ears and you'll hear the voice beyond words - close your senses and you'll experience the realization beyond realizations. In this realization there is neither birth nor death, neither beginning nor end, neither self nor other - in this realization, all is one, one is all. In this realization my heart is yours, your heart is mine - in this realization, you are me, I am you.

13. When Love Awakens
(The Sonnet)

When Love Awakens
(The Sonnet)

When love awakens so will the world,
For love is the seed of civilization.
When love awakens the conflicts will end,
For love is the gateway to assimilation.
When care crosses family suffering will wither,
For selfishness is the cause of miseries.
When the soul is clear enough to reflect all,
All separation will turn into memories.
When breath of one becomes the breath of all,
All atrocious walls will collapse into dust.
When there's no more 'my people your people',
Only then we will be human at last.
When the fire of love engulfs our whole being,
Time will bear witness to humanity's uprising.

14. Instrument of Love

There is no mechanical road to the heart - the heart is the road. It is the road to inclusion - it is the road to equality - it is the road to justice. Why don't you walk on it my friend - because you are impatient - nay, the self in you is impatient. There are two selves in us, one is impatient because it knows it's mortal, another is patient because it knows it's immortal. Know that you live not in flesh and blood but in memories, and you'll be free, you'll be united with all, you'll be one with the whole of humankind.

Death of the self is union with the world. And once you are one with the world what power do the puny labels of society have over you - none. It is this simple - a nonsectarian world starts with a nonsectarian individual. If the world is degraded it may not be my fault, but if it stays that way, it'll be my fault - my fault as in the fault of the individual. Someone has to stand up to lift the world up. Someone has to stand up to lift others up.

In doing so keep your mouth shut unless it's absolutely necessary to open it and let your hands and feet do all the talking. Let actions talk not words. And remember, life is too short to plant anything else but love. A life of hate is the same as a thousand deaths and a death in love is worth a thousand lives. So die my friend, die in love so that you may live for eternity in the heart of humanity.

All puny flames of intellect look bright till the sun of love rises. Walk past your intellect - walk past your faith and let the world be engulfed with your love. A pure heart wide awake with love becomes the very epitome of truth. What is required is love not loyalty. Life is either an instrument of love or nothing at all. Know love and you'll know all. Live love and you'll live for eternity. Work with love as the invisible force of nature so that you may give birth to a new nature

The world is born from the individual - it is born from you. Your light is the world's light, your darkness is the world's darkness. So it is up to you - will you let the world bathe in your light or engulf it with your darkness! The world right now is living in darkness, you know why - because too many people prefer to live in the darkness of indifference than to stand up and let their light shine bright. So the question is, what will your action be?

15. The Loco Sonnet

The Loco Sonnet

Better to be loco for something,
Than to be sane for nothing.
Better to fight and die for a purpose,
Than to sit around and do chanting.
Better to love and be exploited,
Than to be self-obsessed and crooked.
Better to disagree and annoy each other,
Than to hide the differences fostering hatred.
Better to be a know-nothing idiot,
Than to be a know-it-all loudspeaker.
Better a character without fancy clothes,
Than fancy clothes without character.
There's no future without a united humanity.
The whole world is a reflection of me.

16. Real Immortality

I am not here to entertain you or motivate you or lecture you, I am here to make you think - think for our neighborhood, think for our society, think for our world. I am here to point out to you the struggles of the helpless, the hopeless, the forgotten and the destitute, so that you may wake up the human in you and rush to their rescue with all your might and sight.

It is a promise that I ask of you - a promise that no matter the time and age you'll never lose sight of your humanity - you'll never be too immersed in your own comfort to help out those in misery around you. If you can make this promise, not to me mark you but to yourself, then I'll know that I've achieved absolution.

And remember, we don't promise with our lips, we promise with our life. Better lose life than break a promise. Human life is priceless, use it to keep the promise of humanity, not to facilitate the atrocities of inhumanity. Use your senses to serve the people, not the people to serve your senses. Once you do, no power in the world can kill your light. They may kill my body, but how will they kill my soul which lives in the veins of humanitarians across the world!

Person dies, not the values they stand for - not the idea they stand for - not the mission they stand for. There is no such thing as reincarnation of an individual, but one who stands for something greater themselves, never dies from the heart of humanity. Their body dies, but their soul, that is their spirit - the idea behind their life – behind their existence, lives on. The body is only an instrument for the idea - it's the idea that lives not the body.

Soul or spirit can no longer be hailed as some supernatural force that lives on after death - they are mere metaphorical representations of the values, the principles that a person stands for. And often I prefer the terms soul and spirit over their plainer counterparts such as person or individual. Nevertheless, as it turns out, the soul is indeed immortal, but not in the way our ancient ancestors believed it to be.

Our immortality lies in the values we stand for. Our worth is in our values - our worth is in our virtues - our worth is in our principles - without these we are just good-looking savages. Let me simplify this further. I have seen chimpanzees more human than humans. We have a brain full with potential unlike any other species on earth, but having an unparalleled brain makes us no different from other species unless we practice those powers for the benefit of our entire kind.

17. Mind of A Human
(The Sonnet)

Mind of A Human
(The Sonnet)

My kind of dance is the dance of inclusion,
A dance that can't be contained with labels.
My kind of art is the art of assimilation,
An art that is beyond all intellectual fables.
My kind of science is the science of revolution,
A science that is incorruptible by bigotry.
My kind of faith is the faith in egalitarianism,
A faith that is untainted by bookish crookery.
My kind of economics is the economics of equality,
An economics guided by conscience not greed.
My kind of politics is the politics of sanity,
A politics that serves all beyond the politician's need.
I dream of a progress that is not regress in disguise.
Wielding warmth and reason we'll truly rise.

18. Service over Intellect

Humanity needs no name or category - humanity is the world itself - either you are all of it or none of it. There is no salvation for the soul except for existing as the incarnate of all humanity. And one who does is the real human, all others are cheap knockoffs.

If you are not ready to surrender in service at the feet of the helpless, don't tell anyone you are a human. Remember, you cannot find yourself till you lose yourself. In helping others you'll experience the greatest of wisdom. This cannot be comprehended with intellect. An intellectual can never fathom the madness of the humanitarian, for the intellect keeps a person from comprehending the true grandiose of human existence.

Intellect has a tendency to present itself as the authority of society, quite like religion has been doing for millennia. I don't' submit to any authority whatsoever, either intellectual or religious - I don't recognize authority, of someone else or of my own. A being of character and conscience is neither inferior nor superior to anybody else, and as such sees no one as either superior or inferior to themselves. Comparison is the sign of a weak character, those who are strong listen to everyone and learn from everyone. From comparison rises separation, from separation rises conflict, from conflict rises war.

However, here is the fact of the matter. War is in our DNA, so is the capacity for peace. Therefore, the individual must make their choice. The individual must choose in which direction they want to take this world of ours - will they take it down the same rotten path of sectarianism like our ancestors did, or will they build a whole new civilized path - a path that facilitates love, not hate - a path that facilitates discussion, not debate - a path that unites, not divides - in short, a path that is human, not savage!

I myself am the savage and the saint - savagery comes to me easily, sainthood not so much - yet I choose the path of the saint over that of the savage - not because I am some sort of superior being, but because I am an accountable being - I am accountable for what happens to your children and all the children of our world.

19. Mi Humanidad Insiste
(The Sonnet)

Mi Humanidad Insiste
(The Sonnet)

Mi corazón insiste that I can't sit still,
Till the society is human and thus starts living.
Mi corazón insiste that I can't sleep in peace,
Till I bring out the peace the world holds within.
Mi conciencia insiste that I can't stop walking,
Till I make the fallen rise to make their destiny.
Mi conciencia insiste that I can't stop working,
Till each human extends a hand out in solidarity.
Mi alma insiste that my breath is not my own,
Till I breathe life into the souls lost in misery.
Mi alma insiste that I have no right over my veins,
Till the veins of society are freed from disparity.
Mi humanidad insiste the life of one is the life of all.
Either we are one family or nothing at all.

20. Instrument of Peace

Everybody is a sleepy savage except those who are drunk in love for the helpless and the destitute. Love until your body fails. Peace is another name for love. When you learn to love as a truly genuine human ought to love - without expectation, without hope, without the slightest desire for getting back anything, peace will pour in your mind and thereafter out into the world quite on its own.

And that's the way to end all wars - that's the way to end all crime - that's the way to end all inhumanity. Try a crime you end a criminal, treat an environment you end crime - treat, not with intellect but with love - intellect is only a small part of the picture.

The question is - what's stopping you from taking the world in the direction of peace - in the direction of humaneness! What keeps driving you in the path of war - you may say it's society - and yes indeed - it is the society that continues to sustain a savage paradigm that nourishes war instead of fostering peace – but think for a while, what is the society - the society is you - and why do the savageries of the society have to continue through your actions - don't you have a brain - don't you have a spine - why do you have to keep making the same mistakes as our ancestors did - why do you let society drive you in the direction of selfishness and war! Forget what your peers do - break the cycle yourself - don't let the inhumanities continue while you are standing - not on your watch - you are a human, start behaving as such - not as a well-suited cannibal.

Wherever you see bigotry, stand up - wherever you see discrimination, stand up - wherever you see inhumanity, stand up - not out of hate or vengeance, but out of human accountability. Be conscientious, stand strong, and act with responsibility.

You are the gateway to peace - it cannot come from anywhere else. You are the gateway to humanity, it cannot come from anywhere else. If the world doesn't do anything about peace, then to hell with their action - stop relying on the world to make peace, be the peace incarnate for your neighborhood yourself - embody all the peace that you have ever dreamed of for your world - and the world will in time have all the peace it needs.

Rise up and destroy yourself so that you can keep the world from destroying itself. Wake up and sing out loud on top of your voice to the whole world - you may come or not to walk beside me, I won't stand still in silence while the oceans burn and the sun turns dark - I will either right the wrongs or perish in the attempt - and even if I burn to ashes in trying to humanize my surroundings, those ashes of mine will still smoke inclusion, equality and humaneness - I am not born a human to crawl as an indifferent vermin, I am born a human to embrace death for the values, the principles, the virtues that ought to be the foundation of human civilization - I am sleepless and I will stay sleepless till all the children of earth can sleep in peace with a full stomach and a happy heart, without worrying about guns and bombs, without worrying about prejudice and phobia, without worrying about discrimination and deportation - I will stay sleepless till the whole world becomes a family, not in theory, not in philosophy, not in argument, not even in futuristic vision, but in reality and practice.

Forget not, either we are a family or nothing at all. And this family is entrusted to us my friend -

this family is entrusted to us - and till every trace of suffering is wiped out from the face of earth, the struggle must continue - I will die in the struggle - you may die in the struggle - but the struggle must continue.

BIBLIOGRAPHY

Archer M., (2000), Being Human: The Problem of Agency. Cambridge University Press.

Archer M., (2003), Structure, Agency and the Internal Conversation. Cambridge University Press.

Adolphs R (2003) Cognitive neuroscience of human social behaviour. Nature Rev Neurosci 4: 165–178.

Adolphs R, Tranel D, Damasio AR (2003) Dissociable neural systems for recognizing emotions. Brain Cogn 52: 61–69.

Afton, A. D. (1985). Forced copulation as a reproductive strategy of male lesser scaup: A field test of some predictions. - Behaviour 92, p. 146-167.

Allison T, Puce A, McCarthy G. (2000) Social perception from visual cues: role of the STS region. Trends Cogn Sci 4: 267–278.

Andresen, Jensine, and Robert Forman, eds. Cognitive Models and Spiritual Maps. Bowling Green, Ohio: Imprint Academic, 2000.

Ashbrook, James, and Carol Albright. The Humanizing Brain: Where Religion and Neuroscience Meet. Cleveland, OH: Pilgrim Press, 1997.

Azari, Nina, Janpeter Nickel, Gilbert Wunderlich, Michael Niedeggen, Harald Hefter, Lutz Tellmann, Hans Herzog, Petra Stoerig, Dieter Birnbacher, and Rudiger Seitz. "Neural Correlates of Religious Experience." European Journal of Neuroscience 13, no. 8 (2001)

Agar, N. (2004). Liberal eugenics: In defence of human enhancement. London: Blackwell Publishing.

Alteheld, N., Roessler, G., Vobig, M., & Walter, R. (2004). The retina implant new approach to a visual prosthesis. Biomedizinische Technik, 49(4), 99–103.

Antal, A., Nitsche, M. A., Kincses, T. Z., Kruse, W., Hoffmann, K. P., & Paulus, W. (2004a). Facilitation of visuo-motor learning by transcranial direct current stimulation of the motor and extrastriate visual areas in humans. European Journal of Neuroscience, 19(10), 2888–2892.

Bhat Z, Kumar, S, Bhat H (2015) In vitro meat production. Challenges and benefits over conventional meat production. J Sci Food Agric 14: 241–248

Bernstein R. J., (1967), John Dewey. New York: Washington Square Press.

Bernstein R.J., (1971), Praxis and Action: Contemporary Philosophies of Human Activity. Philadelphia: University of Pennsylvania Press.

Bernstein R.J., (1976), The Restructuring Social and Political Thought.

Bernstein R.J., (1983), Beyond Relativism and Objectivism: Science, Hermeneutics, and Praxis. Philadelphia: University of Pennsylvania Press.

Bernstein R.J., (1986), Philosophical Profiles. Philadelphia: University of Pennsylvania Press.

Bernstein R.J., (1991), New Constellation. Cambridge: MIT Press.

Barash, D. P. (1977). Sociobiology of rape in mallards (Anas platyrhynchos): Responses of the mated male. - Science 197, p. 788-789.

Berger, J. (1986). Wild horses of the great basin: Social competition and population size. - The University of Chicago Press, Chicago.

Birkhead, T. R., Johnson, S. D. & Nettleship, D. N. (1985). Extra-pair matings and mate guarding in the common murre Uria aalge. - Anim. Behav. 33, p. 608-619.

Beauregard, Mario, and Vincent Paquette. "Neural Correlates of a Mystical Experience in Carmelite Nuns." Neuroscience Letters 405, no. 3 (2006)

Benson, Herbert. Timeless Healing: The Power and Biology of Belief. New York: Scribner, 1996

Bogen, J.E.(1995a), 'On the neurophysiology of consciousness: Part I. An overview', Consciousness and Cognition, 4.

Bogen, J.E. (1995b), 'On the neurophysiology of consciousness: Part II. Constraining the semantic problem', Consciousness and Cognition, 4.

Bremner, J. D., R. Soufer, et al. (2001). "Gender differences in cognitive and neural correlates of remembrance of emotional words." Psychopharmacol Bull 35 (3).

Brothers, L. (2002). The social brain: A project for integrating primate behavior and neurophysiology in a new domain. In J. T. Cacioppo et al. (Eds.), Foundations in neuroscience. Cambridge, MA: MIT Press.

Buss, D. D. (2003). Evolutionary Psychology: The New Science of Mind, 2nd ed. New York: Allyn & Bacon.

Buss, D. M. (1989). "Conflict between the sexes: Strategic interference and the evocation of anger and upset." J Pers Soc Psychol 56 (5).

Buss, D. M. (1995). "Psychological sex differences. Origins through sexual selection." Am Psychol 50 (3).

Buss, D. M. (2002). "Review: Human Mate Guarding." Neuro Endocrinol Lett 23 (Suppl 4).

Buss, D. M., and D. P. Schmitt (1993). "Sexual strategies theory: An evolutionary perspective on human mating." Psychol Rev 100 (2).

Blakemore SJ, Decety J (2001) From the perception of action to the understanding of intention. Nature Rev Neurosci 2: 561.

Bruce C, Desimone R, Gross CG (1981) Visual properties of neurons in a polysensory area in superior temporal sulcus of the macaque. J Neurophysiol 46: 369–384.

Buccino G, Vogt S, Ritzl A, Fink GR, Zilles K, Freund HJ, Rizzolatti G (2004) Neural circuits underlying imitation of hand actions: an event related fMRI study. Neuron 42: 323–34.

Colapietro V., (1988), "Human Agency: The Habits of Our Being."

Southern Journal of Philosophy, XXVI, 2, pp. 153-68.

Colapietro V., (1992), "Purpose, Power, and Agency." The Monist, 75, 4 (October) pp. 423-44.

Colapietro V., (2003), "Signs and their vicissitudes: Meanings in excess of consciousness and functionality." Logica, Dialogica, Ideologica, a cure di Susan Petrilli e Patrizia Calefato (Milano: Mimesis), pp. 221-36.

Colapietro V., (2004a), "C. S. Peirce's Reclamation of Teleology." Nature in American Philosophy, ed. Jean De Groot (Washington, D.C.: Catholic University Press of America), pp. 88-108.

Colapietro V., (2004b), "Portrait of a Historicist: An Alternative Reading of Peircean Semiotic." Semiotiche, 2/04 [maggio 2004], pp. 49-68.

Colapietro V., (2006), "Engaged Pluralism: Between Alterity and

Sociality." The Pragmatic Century: Conversations with Richard J. Bernstein (Albany, NY: SUNY Press), pp. 39-68.

Colapietro V., (2009), "Habit, Competence, and Purpose." Forthcoming in The Transactions of the Charles S. Peirce Society. Calder AJ, Keane J, Manes F, Antoun N, Young AW (2000) Impaired recognition and experience of disgust following brain injury. Nature Neurosci 3: 1077–1078.

Carey DP, Perrett DI, Oram MW (1997) Recognizing, understanding and reproducing actions. In: Jeannerod M, Grafman J (eds) Handbook of neuropsychology. Vol. 11: Action and cognition. Elsevier, Amsterdam.

Carr L, Iacoboni M, Dubeau MC, Mazziotta JC, Lenzi GL (2003) Neural mechanisms of empathy in humans: a relay from neural systems for imitation to limbic areas. Proc Natl Acad Sci USA 100: 5497–5502.

Changeux JP, Ricoeur P (1998) La nature et la règle. Odile Jacob, Paris.

Cochin S, Barthelemy C, Roux S, Martineau J (1999) Observation and execution of movement: similarities demonstrated by quantified electroencephalograpy. Eur J Neurosci 11: 1839– 1842.

Chomsky Noam, (2017) Requiem for the American Dream

Chomsky Noam, (2016) Who Rules the World?

Chomsky Noam, (2010) How the World Works

Churchland, P.S. (1986), Neurophilosophy (Cambridge, MA: The MIT Press).

Churchland, P.S. & Ramachandran, V.S. (1993), 'Filling in: Why Dennett is wrong', in Dennett and His Critics:

Demystifying Mind, ed. B. Dahlbom (Oxford: Blackwell Scientific Press).

Churchland, P.S., Ramachandran, V.S. & Sejnowski, T.J. (1994), 'A critique of pure vision', in Large- scale Neuronal Theories of the Brain, ed. C. Koch & J.L. Davis (Cambridge, MA: The MIT Press).

Crick, F. (1994), The Astonishing Hypothesis: The Scientific Search for the Soul (New York: Simon and Schuster).

Crick, F. (1996), 'Visual perception: rivalry and consciousness', Nature, 379.

Crick, F. & Koch, C. (1992), 'The problem of consciousness', Scientific American, 267.

Craig AD (2002) How do you feel? Interoception: the sense of the physiological condition of the body. Nature Rev Neurosci 3: 655–666.

Damasio, A (2003a) Looking for Spinoza. Harcourt Inc. Damasio A (2003b) Feeling of emotion and the self. Ann NY Acad Sci 1001: 253–261.

d'Aquili, Eugene. "Senses of Reality in Science and Religion." Zygon 17, no 4 (1982)

d'Aquili, Eugene. "The Biopsychological Determinants of Religious Ritual Behavior." Zygon 10, no. 1 (1975)

d'Aquili, Eugene. "The Myth-Ritual Complex: A Biogenetic Structural Analysis." Zygon 18, no. 3 (1983)

d'Aquili, Eugene, and Andrew Newberg. The Mystical Mind: Probing the Biology of Religious Experience. Minneapolis: Fortress Press, 1999.

Daly DD. 1958. Ictal affect. Am J Psychiatry.

Damasio, A. (1994) Descartes' Error: Emotion, Reason and the Human Brain. New York, Putnams.

Damasio, A. (1999) The Feeling of What Happens: Body, Emotion and the Making of Consciousness. London, Heinemann.

Darwin, C. (1859) On the Origin of Species by Means of Natural Selection. London, Murray.

Darwin, C. (1871) The Descent of Man and Selection in Relation to Sex. London, John Murray.

Darwin, C. (1872) The Expression of the Emotions in Man and Animals. London, John Murray; also published 1965, Chicago, University of Chicago Press.

Dawkins, M.S. (1987) Minding and mattering. In C. Blakemore and S. Greenfield (eds) Mindwaves. Oxford, Blackwell, 151-60.

Dawkins, R. (1976) The Selfish Gene. Oxford, Oxford University Press; a new edition, with additional material, was published in 1989.

Dawkins, R. (1986) The Blind Watchmaker. London, Longman.

Di Pellegrino G, Fadiga L, Fogassi L, Gallese V, Rizzolatti G (1992) Understanding motor events: A neurophysiological study. Exp Brain Res 91: 176–80.

Deikman, A.J. (2000) A functional approach to mysticism. Journal of Consciousness Studies 7(11-12), 75-91.

Delmonte, M.M. (1987) Personality and meditation. In M. West (ed.) The Psychology of Meditation. Oxford, Clarendon Press, 118-32.

Dennett, D.C. (1987) The Intentional Stance. Cambridge, MA, MIT Press.

Dennett, D.C. (1988) Quining qualia. In A.J. Marcel and E. Bisiach (eds)

Consciousness in Contemporary Science. Oxford, Oxford University Press, 42-77.

Dennett, D.C. (1991) Consciousness Explained. Boston, MA, and London, Little, Brown and Co.

Dennett, D.C. (1995a) Darwin's Dangerous Idea. London, Penguin.

Dennett, D.C. (1995b) The unimagined preposterousness of zombies. Journal of Consciousness Studies 2(4), 322-6.

Dennett, D.C. (1995c) Cog: steps towards consciousness in robots. In T. Metzinger (ed.) Conscious Experience. Thorverton, Devon, Imprint Academic, 471-87.

Dennett, D.C. (1995d) The path not taken. Behavioral and Brain Sciences 18, 252-3; commentary on N. Block, On a confusion about a function of consciousness. Behavioral and Brain Sciences 18, 227.

Dennett, D.C. (1996a) Facing backwards on the problem of consciousness. Journal of Consciousness Studies 3(1), 4-6.

Dennett, D.C. (1996b) Kinds of Minds: Towards an Understanding of Consciousness. London, Weidenfeld & Nicolson.

Dennett, D.C. (1997) An exchange with Daniel Dennett. In J. Searle (ed.) The Mystery of Consciousness. New York, New York Review of Books, 115-19.

Dennett, D.C. (1998) The myth of double transduction. In S.R. Hameroff, A.W. Kaszniak and A. C. Scott (eds) Toward a Science of Consciousness: The Second Tucson Discussions and Debates. Cambridge, MA, MIT Press, 97-107.

Dennett, D.C. (1998b) Brainchildren: Essays on Designing Minds. Cambridge, MA, MIT Press.

Dennett, D.C. (2001) The fantasy of first person science. Debate with D. Chalmers, Northwestern University, Evanston, IL, February 2001.

Dennett, D.C. (2003) Freedom Evolves. New York, Penguin.

Dennett, D.C. and Kinsbourne, M. (1992) Time and the observer: the where and when of consciousness in the brain. Behavioral and Brain Sciences 15, 183-247, including commentaries and authors' responses.

Dewey J., (1911 [1977]), "Epistemological Realism: The Alleged Ubiquity of the Knowledge Relation." Journal of Philosophy, VIII, 20 (September 28, 1911).

Dewhurst, Kenneth, and A. W. Beard. "Sudden Religious Conversions in Temporal Lobe Epilepsy." British Journal of Psychiatry 117 (1970)

Dewhurst K, Beard AW. Sudden religious conversions in temporal lobe epilepsy. 1970 Epilepsy Behav 2003

Devinsky O, Lai G. Spirituality and religion in epilepsy. Epilepsy Behav 2008.

Devinsky, O., Morrell, MJ, Vogt, BA. (1995) 'Contribution of anterior cingulate cortex to behavior', Brain, 118.

Douglas Stone A., Chapter 24, The Indian Comet, in the book Einstein and the Quantum, Princeton University Press, Princeton, New Jersey, 2013.

E. Horvitz, "One Hundred Year Study on Artificial Intelligence: Reflections and Framing," ed: Stanford University, 2014.

Einstein A. (1925). "Quantentheorie des einatomigen idealen Gases". Sitzungsberichte der Preussischen Akademie der Wissenschaften.

Eckhart Meister, Selected Writings

Egidi R., ed. (1999), "Von Wright and 'Dante's Dream': Stages in a Philosophical Pilgrim's Progress", in In Search of a New Humanism: the Philosophy of G.H. von Wright, ed. by R. Egidi, Kluwer, Dordrecht.

Fadiga L, Fogassi L, Pavesi G, Rizzolatti G (1995) Motor facilitation during action observation: a magnetic stimulation study. J Neurophysiol 73: 2608–2611.

Fogassi L, Gallese V, Fadiga L, Rizzolatti G (1998) Neurons responding to the sight of goal directed hand/arm actions in the parietal area PF (7b) of the macaque monkey. Soc Neurosci Abs 24:257.5.

Frith U, Frith CD (2003) Development and neurophysiology of mentalizing. Philos Trans R Soc Lond B Biol Sci 358: 459.

Farah, M.J. (1989), 'The neural basis of mental imagery', Trends in Neurosciences, 10.

Finlay BL, Darlington RB (1995) Linked regularities in the development and evolution of mammalian brains. Science 268.

Freud, S. "The Interpretation of Dreams", 1900

Freud, S. "Selected papers on hysteria and other psychoneuroses" Journal of Nervous and Mental Disease 1909.

Freud, S. "The Origin and Development of Psychoanalysis", 1910

Freud, S. "Psychopathology of everyday life", 1914

Freud, S. "Beyond the Pleasure Principle", 1920

Frith, C.D. & Dolan, R.J. (1997), 'Abnormal beliefs: Delusions and memory', Paper presented at the May,

1997, Harvard Conference on Memory and Belief.

Gay, Volney, ed. Neuroscience and Religion. Plymouth, UK: Lexington Books, 2009.

Gazzaniga, M. S. (1985). The social brain. New York: Basic Books.

Gazzaniga, M.S. (1993), 'Brain mechanisms and conscious experience', Ciba Foundation Symposium, 174.

Geschwind N. "Behavioural changes in temporal lobe epilepsy". Psychol Med. 1979.

Gellhorn, E., Kiely, W.F. "Mystical states of consciousness: neurophysiological and clinical aspects." J Nerv Ment Dis. 1972;154:399-405.

Gilbert SL, Dobyns WB, Lahn BT (2005) Genetic links between brain development and brain evolution. Nat Rev Genet 6.

Gray JA. The Psychology of Fear and Stress. 2nd ed. New York, NY: Cambridge University Press; 1988.

Gloor, P. (1992), 'Amygdala and temporal lobe epilepsy', in The Amygdala: Neurobiological Aspects of Emotion, Memory and Mental Dysfunction, ed J.P. Aggleton (New York: Wiley-Liss).

Greenspan, S. I. and S. G. Shanker (2004). The first idea: How symbols, language, and intelligence evolved from our early primate ancestors to modern humans. Cambridge, MA: Da Capo Press.

Grady, D. (1993), 'The vision thing: Mainly in the brain', Discover, June.

Gallagher HL, Frith CD (2003) Functional imaging of 'theory of mind'. Trends Cogn Sci 7: 77.

Gallese V, Fogassi L, Fadiga L, Rizzolatti G (2002) Action representation and the inferior parietal lobule. In: Prinz W, Hommel B (eds) Attention & Performance XIX. Common mechanisms in perception and action. Oxford University Press, Oxford.

Gallese V, Keysers C, Rizzolatti G (2004) A unifying view of the basis of social cognition. Trends Cogn Sci 8: 396–403.

Gangitano M, Mottaghy FM, Pascual-Leone A (2001) Phase specific modulation of cortical motor output during movement observation. NeuroReport 12: 1489–1492.

Gangitano M, Mottaghy FM, Pascual-Leone A (2004) Modulation of premotor mirror neuron activity during observation of unpredictable grasping movements. Eur J Neurosci 20: 2193– 2202.

Goldman AI, Sripada CS (2004) Simulationist models of face-based emotion recognition. Cognition 94: 193–213.

Grèzes J, Costes N, Decety J (1998) Top-down effect of strategy on the perception of human biological motion: a PET investigation. Cogn Neuropsychol 15: 553–582.

Grèzes J, Armony JL, Rowe J, Passingham RE (2003) Activations related to "mirror" and "canonical" neurones in the human brain: an fMRI study. Neuroimage 18: 928–937.

Gross CG, Rocha-Miranda CE, Bender DB (1972) Visual properties of neurons in the inferotemporal cortex of the macaque. J Neurophysiol 35: 96–111.

Hari R, Forss N, Avikainen S, Kirveskari S, Salenius S, Rizzolatti G (1998) Activation of human primary motor cortex during action observation: a neuromagnetic study.

Proc. Natl Acad Sci USA 95: 15061–15065.

Hardy, G. H. (1940). Ramanujan. Cambridge: Cambridge University Press.

Hall, Daniel, Keith Meador, and Harold Koenig. "Measuring Religiousness in Health Research: Review and Critique." Journal of Religion and Health 47, no. 2 (2008)

Harris, Sam, Jonas Kaplan, Ashley Curiel, Susan Bookheimer, Marco Iacoboni, and Mark Cohen. "The Neural Correlates of Religious and Nonreligious Belief." PLoS One 4, no. 10 (October 1, 2009)

Halgren, E. (1992), 'Emotional neurophysiology of the amygdala within the context of human cognition', in The Amygdala: Neurobiological Aspects of Emotion, Memory and Mental Dysfunction, ed J.P. Aggleton (New York: Wiley-Liss).

Halligan PW, Fink GR, Marshal JC, Vallar G. 2003. Spatial cognition: evidence from visual neglect. Trends Cogn Sci.

Handbook of Emotions, Edited by Michael Lewis, Jeannette M. Haviland-Jones, and Lisa Feldman Barrett, The Guilford Press; 3rd edition (2010).

Haggard, P., Clark, S. and Kalogeras,]. (2002) Voluntary action and conscious awareness, Nature Neuroscience 5, 382-5. Haggard, P., Newman, C. and Magno, E. (1999) On the perceived time of voluntary actions. British Journal of Psychology 90, 291-303.

Hameroff, S.R. and Penrose, R. (1996) Conscious events as orchestrated space-time selections. Journal of Consciousness Studies 3(1), 36-53; also reprinted in J. Shear (ed.) (1997) Explaining Consciousness-The Hard Problem. Cambridge, MA, MIT Press, 177-95.

Hardcastle, V.G. (2000) How to understand theN in NCC. InT. Metzinger (ed.) Neural Correlates of Consciousness. Cambridge, MA, MIT Press, 259-64.

Harding, D.E. (1961) On Having no Head: Zen and the Re-Discovery of the Obvious. London, Buddhist Society.

Hardy, A. (1979) The Spiritual Nature of Man: A Study of Contemporary Religious Experience. Oxford, Clarendon Press.

Hamad, S. (1990) The symbol grounding problem. Physica D 42, 335-46.

Hamad, S. (2001) No easy way out. The Sciences 41(2), 36-42.

Harre, R. and Gillett, G. (1994) The Discursive Mind. Thousand Oaks, CA, Sage.

Haugeland, J. (ed.) (1997) Mind Design II: Philosophy, Psychology, Artificial

Intelligence. Cambridge, MA, MIT Press.

Hauser, M.D. (2000) Wild Minds: What Animals Really Think. New York, Henry Holt and Co.; London, Penguin.

Hearne, K. (1990) The Dream Machine. Northants, Aquarian.

Hebb, D.O. (1949) The Organization of Behavior. New York, Wiley.

Helmholtz, H.L.F. von (1856-67) Treatise on Physiological Optics.

Hess, EH (1975) "The role of pupil size in communication," Scientific American, 233(5), 110–12.

Heyes, C.M. (1998) Theory of mind in nonhuman primates. Behavioral and Brain Sciences 21, 101-48; with commentaries.

Heyes, C.M. and Galef, B.G. (eds) (1996) Social Learning in Animals: The Roots of Culture. San Diego, CA, Academic Press.

Hilgard, E.R. (1986) Divided Consciousness: Multiple Controls in Human Thought and Action. New York, Wiley.

Hocquette JF (2016) Is in vitro meat the solution for the future? Meat Science 120:

167–176

Hodgson, R. (1891) A case of double consciousness. Proceedings of the Society for Psychical Research 7, 221-58.

Hofstadter, D.R. (1979) Code!, Escher, Bach: An Eternal Golden Braid. London, Penguin.

Hofstadter, D.R. and Dennett, D.C. (eds) (1981) The Mind's I: Fantasies and Reflections on Self and Soul. London, Penguin.

Holland, J. (ed.) (2001) Ecstasy: The Complete Guide: A Comprehensive Look at the Risks and Benefits of

MDMA. Rochester, VT, Park Street Press.

Holmes, D.S. (1987) The influence of meditation versus rest on physiological arousal. In M. West (ed.) The Psychology of Meditation. Oxford, Clarendon Press, 81-103.

Holt, J. (1999) Blindsight in debates about qualia. Journal of Consciousness Studies 6(5), 54-71.

Horgan, J. (1994), 'Can science explain consciousness?', Scientific American, 271.

Holloway RL (1996) Evolution of the human brain. In: Lock A, Peters CR (eds) Handbook of human symbolic evolution. Oxford University Press, Oxford

Iacoboni M, Woods RP, Brass M, Bekkering H, Mazziotta JC, Rizzolatti G (1999) Cortical mechanisms of human imitation. Science 286: 2526–2528.

Iacoboni M, Koski LM, Brass M, Bekkering H, Woods RP, Dubeau MC, Mazziotta JC, Rizzolatti G (2001) Reafferent copies of imitated actions in the right superior temporal cortex. Proc Natl Acad Sci USA 98: 13995–13999.

Jeannerod M (1988) The neural and behavioural organization of goal-directed movements. Clarendon Press, Oxford.

Johnson-Frey SH, Maloof FR, Newman-Norlund R, Farrer C, Inati S, Grafton ST (2003) Actions or hand-objects interactions? Human inferior frontal cortex and action observation. Neuron 39: 1053–1058.

Jackson, F. (1982) Epiphenomenal qualia. Philosophical Quarterly 32, 127-36.

James, W. (1890) The Principles of Psychology (2 volumes). London, Macmillan.

James, W. (1902) The Varieties of Religious Experience: A Study in Human Nature. New York and London, Longmans, Green and Co.

Jansen, K. (2001) Ketamine: Dreams and Realities. Sarasota, FL, Multidisciplinary Association for Psychedelic Studies.

Jay, M. (ed.) (1999) Artificial Paradises: A Drugs Reader. London, Penguin.

Jaynes, J. (1976) The Origin of Consciousness in the Breakdown of the Bicameral Mind. New York, Houghton Mifflin.

Johnson, M.K. and Raye, C.L. (1981) Reality monitoring. Psychological Review 88, 67-85.

Kadim I, Mahgoub O, Baqir S et al. (2015) Cultured meat from muscle stem cells: a review of challenges and prospects. J Integr Agr 14: 222–233

Koski L, Iacoboni M, Dubeau MC, Woods RP, Mazziotta JC (2003) Modulation of cortical activity during different imitative behaviors. J Neurophysiol 89: 460–471.

Krolak-Salmon P, Henaff MA, Isnard J, Tallon-Baudry C, Guenot M, Vighetto A, Bertrand O, Mauguiere F (2003) An attention modulated response to disgust in human ventral anterior insula. Ann Neurol 53: 446–453.

Kandel, E. R. In Search of Memory: The Emergence of a New Science of Mind, W. W. Norton & Company (2007).

Kandel E. R. Schwartz JH, Jessel TM. Principles of neural sciences. New York; McGraw Hill, 2000.

Kanizsa, G. (1979), Organization In Vision (New York: Praeger).

Kaloupek DG, Scott JR, Khatami V. Assessment of coping strategies associated with syncope in blood donors. J Psychosom Res. 1985;29:207-214.

Kanwisher, N. (2001) Neural events and perceptual awareness. Cognition 79, 89-113; also reprinted inS. Dehaene (ed.) The Cognitive Neuroscience of Consciousness. Cambridge, MA, MIT Press, 89-113.

Kapleau, Roshi P. (1980) The Three Pillars of Zen: Teaching, Practice, and Enlightenment (revised edn). New York, Doubleday.

Karn, K. and Hayhoe, M. (2000) Memory representations guide targeting eye movements in a natural task. Visual Cognition 7, 673-703.

Kasamatsu, A. and Hirai, T. (1966) An electroencephalographic study on the Zen meditation (zazen). Folia Psychiatrica et Neurologica Japonica 20, 315-36.

Kaiserman-Abramof, I. R., Graybiel, A. M., & Nauta, W. J. (1980). The thalamic projection to cortical area 17 in a congenitally anophthalmic mouse strain. Neuroscience, 5, 41–52.

Kanold, P. O., Kara, P., Reid, R. C., & Shatz, C. J. (2003). Role of subplate neurons in functional maturation of visual cortical columns. Science, 301, 521–525.

Kennedy, H., & Dehay, C. (1988). Functional implications of the anatomical organization of the callosal projections of visual areas V1 and V2 in the macaque monkey. Behav. Brain Res., 29, 225–236.

Kentridge, R.W. and Heywood, C.A. (1999) The status of blindsight. Journal of Consciousness Studies 6(5), 3-11.

Kihlstrom, J.F. (1996) Perception without awareness of what is perceived, learning without awareness of what is learned. In M. Velmans (ed.) The Science of Consciousness. London, Routledge, 23-46.

Kollerstrom, N. (1999) The path of Halley's comet, and Newton's late apprehension of the law of gravity. Annals of Science 56, 331-56.

Kosslyn, S.M. (1980) Image and Mind. Cambridge, MA, Harvard University Press.

Kosslyn, S.M. (1988) Aspects of a cognitive neuroscience of mental imagery. Science 240, 1621-6.

Kinsbourne, M. (1995), 'The intralaminar thalamic nucleii', Consciousness and Cognition, 4.

Kjaer, Troels, Camilla Bertelsen, Paola Piccini, David Brooks, Jorgen Alving, and Hans Lou. "Increased Dopamine Tone during Meditation- Induced Change of Consciousness." Cognitive Brain Research 13, no. 2 (April 2002)

Kölmel HW. 1985. Complex visual hallucinations in the hemianopic field. J Neurol Neurosurg Psychiatry.

Koenig, Harold. "Research on Religion, Spirituality, and Mental Health: A Review." Canadian Journal of Psychiatry 54, no. 5 (May 2009)

Koenig, Harold, ed. Handbook of Religion and Mental Health. San Diego, CA: Academic Press, 1998

Kraepelin E. Psychiatry: A Textbook for Students and Physicians. New York, NY: Science History Publications; 1990.

Lauglin, Charles, John McManus, and Eugene d'Aquili. Brain, Symbol, and Experience. 2nd ed. New York: Columbia University Press, 1992

Lakoff, G. and M. Johnson (1999). Philosophy in the flesh. Basic Books: New York.

LeDoux, J. E. (1996). The emotional brain. New York: Simon & Schuster.

LeDoux, J.E. (1992), 'Emotion and the amygdala', in The Amygdala:

Neurobiological Aspects of Emo- tion, Memory and Mental Dysfunction, ed J.P. Aggleton (New York: Wiley-Liss).

Levin, D.T. and Simons, D.J. (1997) Failure to detect changes to attended objects in motion pictures. Psychonomic Bulletin and Review 4, 501-6.

Levine,J. (1983) Materialism and qualia: the explanatory gap. Pacific Philosophical Quarterly 64, 354-61.

Levine,J. (2001) Purple Haze: The Puzzle of Consciousness. New York, Oxford University Press. Levine, S. (1979) A Gradual Awakening. New York, Doubleday.

Levinson, B.W. (1965) States of awareness during general anaesthesia. British Journal of Anaesthesia 37, 544-6.

Lewicki, P., Czyzewska, M. and Hoffman, H. (1987) Unconscious acquisition of complex procedural knowledge. Journal of Experimental Psychology: Learning, Memory and Cognition 13, 523-30.

Lewicki, P., Hill, T. and Bizot, E. (1988) Acquisition of procedural knowledge about a pattern of stimuli that cannot be articulated. Cognitive Psychology 20, 24-37.

Lewicki, P., Hill, T. and Czyzewska, M. (1992) Nonconscious acquisition of information. American Psychologist 47, 796-801.

Manthey S, Schubotz RI, von Cramon DY (2003). Premotor cortex in observing erroneous action: an fMRI study. Brain Res Cogn Brain Res 15: 296–307.

Mesulam MM, Mufson EJ (1982) Insula of the old world monkey. III: Efferent cortical output and comments on function. J Comp Neurol 212: 38–52.

Naskar, Abhijit. "Homo: A Brief History of Consciousness", 2015

Naskar, Abhijit. "What is Mind?", 2016

Naskar, Abhijit. "Love, God & Neurons: Memoir of A Scientist who found himself by getting lost", 2016

Naskar, Abhijit. "Principia Humanitas", 2017

Naskar, Abhijit. "We Are All Black: A Treatise on Racism", 2017

Naskar, Abhijit. "Either Civilized or Phobic: A Treatise on Homosexuality", 2017

Naskar, Abhijit. "I Am The Thread: My Mission", 2017

Naskar, Abhijit. "The Bengal Tigress: A Treatise on Gender Equality", 2017

Naskar, Abhijit. "Morality Absolute", 2017

Naskar, Abhijit. "Build Bridges not Walls: In the name of Americana", 2018

Naskar, Abhijit. "Fabric of Humanity", 2018

Naskar, Abhijit. "Lives To Serve Before I Sleep", 2019

Naskar, Abhijit. "Citizens of Peace: Beyond the Savagery of Sovereignty", 2019

Naskar, Abhijit. "The Constitution of The United Peoples of Earth", 2019

Naskar, Abhijit. "Neurons Giveth, Neurons Taketh Away | Abhijit Naskar | TEDxIIMRanchi", 2019 https://www.youtube.com/watch?v=BNX-Q0ySm80

Naskar, Abhijit. "Mission Reality", 2019

Naskar, Abhijit. "Operation Justice: To Make A Society That Needs No Law", 2019

Naskar, Abhijit. "Every Generation Needs Caretakers: The Gospel of Patriotism", 2020

Naskar, Abhijit. "Revolution Indomable", 2020

Naskar, Abhijit. "Servitude is Sanctitude", 2020

Naskar, Abhijit. "Good Scientist: When Science and Service Combine", 2020

Newberg, Andrew, and Jeremy Iversen. "The Neural Basis of the Complex Mental Task of Meditation: Neurotransmitter and Neurochemical Considerations." Medical Hypotheses 61, no. 2 (2003).

Newberg, Andrew. "How God Changes Your Brain: An Introduction to Jewish Neurotheology", CCAR Journal: The Reform Jewish Quarterly, Winter 2016.

Newberg, Andrew, and Stephanie Newberg. "A Neuropsychological Perspective on Spiritual Development." In Handbook of Spiritual Development in Childhood and Adolescence, edited by Eugene

Roehlkepartain, Pamela King, Linda Wagener, and Peter Benson. London: Sage Publications, Inc., 2005

Newberg, Andrew. "The Neurotheology Link An Intersection Between Spirituality and Health", Alternative and Complimentary Therapies, Vol 21 No 1, February 2015.

Newberg, Andrew, Nancy Wintering, Dharma Khalsa, Hannah Roggenkamp, and Mark Waldman. "Meditation Effects on Cognitive Function and Cerebral Blood Flow in Subjects with Memory Loss: A Preliminary Study." Journal of Alzheimer's Disease 20, no. 2 (2010)

Nash, M. (1995), 'Glimpses of the mind', Time.

Nesse RM. Proximate and evolutionary studies of anxiety, stress and depression: synergy at the interface. Neurosci Biobehav Rev. 1999;23:895-903.

Nicolelis, Miguel. (2011) "Beyond Boundaries: The New Neuroscience of Connecting Brains with Machines---and How It Will Change Our Lives", Times Books

O'Hara, K. and Scutt, T. (1996) There is no hard problem of consciousness. Journal of Consciousness Studies 3(4), 290-302, reprinted in J. Shear (ed.) (1997) Explaining Consciousness. Cambridge, MA, MIT Press, 69-82.

O'Regan, J.K. (1992) Solving the "real" mysteries of visual perception: the world as an outside memory. Canadian Journal of Psychology 46, 461-88.

O'Regan, J.K. and Noe, A. (2001) A sensorimotor account of vision and visual consciousness. Behavioral and Brain Sciences 24(5), 883-917.

O'Regan, J.K., Rensink, R.A. and Clark,].]. (1999) Change-blindness as a result of "mudsplashes." Nature 398, 34.

Ornstein, R.E. (1977) The Psychology of Consciousness (2nd edn). New York, Harcourt.

Ornstein, R.E. (1986) The Psychology of Consciousness (3rd edn). New York, Pehguin.

Ornstein, R.E. (1992) The Evolution of Consciousness. New York, Touchstone.

Penfield W, Faulk ME (1955) The insula: further observations on its function. Brain 78: 445– 470.

Penrose, R. (1994), Shadows of the Mind (Oxford: Oxford University Press).

Penrose, R. (1989), The Emperor's New Mind: Concerning Computers, Minds and The Laws of Physics (Oxford: Oxford University Press).

Persinger, "'I would kill in God's name' role of sex, weekly church attendance, report of a religious experience and limbic lability" Perceptual and Motor Skills 1997.

Persinger "Experimental simulation of the God experience" Neurotheology 2003.

Persinger, M. A. (1993b). Personality changes following brain injury as a grief response to the loss of sense of self: Phenomenological themes as indices of local lability and neurocognitive restructuring as psycho- therapy. Psychological Reports, 72

Persinger, Corradini, Clement, Keaney, et al "Neurotheology and its convergence with neuroquantology" NeuroQuantology 2010.

Persinger, Koren and St-Pierre "The electromagnetic induction of mystical and altered states within the laboratory" Journal of Consciousness Exploration and Research 2010.

Persinger "Case report: A prototypical spontaneous 'sensed presence' of a sentient being and concomitant electroencephalographic activity in the clinical laboratory" Neurocase 2008.

Persinger and Saroka "Potential production of Hughlings Jackson's "parasitic consciousness" by physiologically-patterned weak transcerebral magnetic fields: QEEG and source localization" Epilepsy & Behavior 28 (2013).

Persinger. "The neuropsychiatry of paranormal experiences". J Neuropsychiatry Clin Neurosci 2001.

Persinger. "Neuropsychological bases of god beliefs", New York: Praeger, 1987

Persinger. "Temporal lobe epileptic signs and correlative behaviors displayed by normal populations", Journal of General Psychology, 1986

Perry BD, Pollard R. Homeostasis, stress, trauma, and adaptation. A neurodevelopmental view of childhood trauma. Child Adolesc Psychiatr Clin N Am. 1998;7:33.

Paré, D. & Llinás, R. (1995), 'Conscious and preconscious processes as seen from the standpoint of sleep-waking cycle neurophysiology', Neuropsychologia, 33.

P. S. de Laplace. Essai Philosophique sur les Probabilites [1814], in Academy des Sciences, Oeuvres Complotes de Laplace, Vol. 7, Gauthier-Villars, Paris (1886).

Perrett DI, Harries MH, Bevan R, Thomas S, Benson PJ, Mistlin AJ, Chitty AJ, Hietanen JK, Ortega JE (1989) Frameworks of analysis for the neural representation of animate objects and actions. J Exp Bio 146: 87–113.

Phillips ML, Young AW, Senior C, Brammer M, Andrew C, Calder AJ, Bullmore ET, Perrett DI, Rowland D, Williams SC, Gray JA, David AS (1997) A specific neural substrate for perceiving facial expressions of disgust. Nature 389: 495–498.

Phillips ML, Young AW, Scott SK, Calder AJ, Andrew C, Giampietro V, Williams SC, Bullmore ET, Brammer M, Gray JA (1998) Neural responses to facial and vocal expressions of fear and disgust. Proc R Soc Lond B Biol Sci 265: 1809–1817.

Puce A, Perrett D (2003) Electrophysiological and brain imaging of biological motion. Philosoph Trans Royal Soc Lond, Series B, 358: 435–445.

Ramachandran VS. Behavioral and magnetoencephalographic correlates of plasticity in the adult human brain. Proc Natl Acad Sci USA 1993; 90: 10413–20.

Ramachandran VS. Phantom limbs, neglect syndromes, repressed memories, and Freudian psychology. Int Rev Neurobiol 1994; 37: 291–333.

Ramachandran VS. Plasticity and functional recovery in neurology. Clin Med 2005; 5: 368–73.

Ramachandran VS, Hirstein W. The perception of phantom limbs. The D. O. Hebb lecture. Brain 1998; 121: 1603–30.

Ramachandran VS, Rogers-Ramachandran D, Cobb S. Touching the phantom limb. Nature 1995; 377: 489–90.

Ramachandran VS, Rogers-Ramachandran D. Phantom limbs and neural plasticity. Arch Neurol 2000; 57: 317–20.

Ramachandran VS, Rogers-Ramachandran D. It's all done with mirrors. Sci Am Mind 2007; 18: 16–9.

Ramachandran VS, Rogers-Ramachandran D. Sensations referred to a patient's phantom arm from another subjects intact arm: perceptual correlates of mirror neurons. Med Hypotheses 2008; 70: 1233–4.

Ramachandran VS, Rogers-Ramachandran D, Stewart M. Perceptual correlates of massive cortical reorganization. Science 1992; 258: 1159–60.

Rizzolatti G, Craighero L (2004) The mirror-neuron system. Annu Rev Neurosci 27: 169–192.

Rizzolatti G, Fogassi L, Gallese V (2001) Neurophysiological mechanisms underlying the understanding and imitation of action. Nature Rev Neurosci 2:661–670.

Rock I, Victor J. Vision and touch: an experimentally created conflict between the two senses. Science 1964; 143: 594–6.

Rose′n B, Lundborg G. Training with a mirror in rehabilitation of the hand. Scand J Plast Reconstr Surg Hand Surg 2005; 39: 104–8.

Royet JP, Plailly J, Delon-Martin C, Kareken DA, Segebarth C (2003) fMRI of emotional responses to odors: influence of hedonic valence and judgment, handedness, and gender. Neuroimage 20: 713–728.

Rozin R Haidt J and McCauley CR (2000) Disgust. In: Lewis M, Haviland-Jones JM (eds) Handbook of Emotion. 2nd Edition. Guilford Press, New York, pp 637–653.

Saxe R, Carey S, Kanwisher N (2004) Understanding other minds: linking developmental psychology and functional neuroimaging. Annu Rev Psychol 55: 87–124.

S. J. Russell and P. Norvig, Artificial intelligence: a modern approach (3rd edition): Prentice Hall, 2009.

Schienle A, Stark R, Walter B, Blecker C, Ott U, Kirsch P, Sammer G, Vaitl D (2002) The insula is not specifically involved in disgust processing: an fMRI study. Neuroreport 13: 2023–2026.

Showers MJC, Lauer EW (1961) Somatovisceral motor patterns in the insula. J Comp Neurol 117: 107–115.

Singer T, Seymour B, O'Doherty J, Kaube H, Dolan RJ, Frith CD (2004) Empathy for pain involves the affective but not the sensory components of pain. Science 303: 1157–1162.

Smith A (1759) The theory of moral sentiments (ed. 1976). Clarendon Press, Oxford.

S. N. Bose (1924). "Plancks Gesetz und Lichtquantenhypothese". Zeitschrift für Physik. 26 (1): 178–181.

Sprengelmeyer R, Rausch M, Eysel UT, Przuntek H (1998) Neural structures associated with recognition of facial expressions of basic emotions Proc R Soc Lond B Biol Sci 265: 1927–1931.

Strafella AP, Paus T (2000) Modulation of cortical excitability during action observation: a transcranial magnetic stimulation study. NeuroReport 11: 2289–2292.

Simonsen R (2015) Eating for the future: veganism and the challenge of in vitro meat. In: Stapleton P, Byers A (Hg). Biopolitics and utopia. Palgrave Macmillan, New York (2015), S 167–190

Tanaka K (1996) Inferotemporal cortex and object vision. Ann Rev Neurosci. 19: 109–140.

Tesla N. "My Inventions", 1919

T. R. Society, "Machine learning: the power and promise of computers that learn by example," ed. The Royal Society, 2017.

Tomasello M, Call J (1997) Primate cognition. Oxford University Press, Oxford.

Tremblay C, Robert M, Pascual-Leone A, Lepore F, Nguyen DK, Carmant L, Bouthillier A, Theoret H (2004) Action observation and execution: intracranial recordings in a human subject. Neurology. 63: 937–938.

Umilta MA, Kohler E, Gallese V, Fogassi L, Fadiga L, Keysers C, Rizzolatti G (2001) "I know what you are doing": a neurophysiological study. Neuron 32: 91–101.

Von Wright G.H., (1963), Norm and Action. A Logical Inquiry, Routledge & Kegan Paul, London.

Von Wright G.H., (1976), "Determinism and the Study of Man", in Essays on Explanation and Understanding, ed. by J. Manninen and R. Tuomela, Reidel, Dordrecht.

Von Wright G.H., (1977), "What is Humanism?", The Lindlay Lecture, University of Arkansas, Lawrence, Kansas.

Von Wright G.H., (1979), "Humanism and the Humanities", in Philosophy and Grammar, ed. by S. Kanger and S. Öhman, Reidel, Dordrecht, pp. 1-16. Reprinted in von Wright (1993).

Von Wright G.H., (1980), Freedom and Determination, North-Holland Publishing Co., Amsterdam.

Von Wright G.H., (1985), Of Human Freedom, The Tanner Lectures on Human Values,

Vol. VI, ed. by S. M. McMurrin, University of Utah Press, Salt Lake City, pp. 107-70. Reprinted in von Wright (1998).

Von Wright G.H., (1993), The Tree of Knowledge and Other Essays, Brill, Leiden.

Von Wright G.H., (1997), "Progress: Fact and Fiction", in The Idea of Progress, ed. by A. Burgen et al., W. de Gruyter, Berlin, pp. 1-18.

Von Wright G.H., (1998), In the Shadow of Descartes: Essays in the Philosophy of Mind, Kluwer, Dordrecht.